GUIDE TO

THAILAND

MICHAEL MARCH

Consultant: Ajarn Somboon Singkamanan

Highlights for Children

CONTENTS

On the cover: This Buddhist temple, with a statue of a seated Buddha in front, is located among trees, lakes, and mountains near Sukhothai, in northern Thailand.

The publisher is grateful for the guidance of the Tourism Authority of Thailand in London, England, and to Ajarn Somboon Singkamanan of Bangkok. She is a senior lecturer of Srinakharinwirot University and a founding member of the Thai International Board on Books for Young People. She is also a well-known storyteller and children's literature specialist.

Published by Highlights for Children
© 2000 Highlights for Children, Inc.
P.O. Box 18201
Columbus, Ohio 43218-0201
For information on *Top Secret Adventures*, visit www.tsadventures.com or call 1-800-962-3661.

10 9 8 7 6 5
ISBN 0-87534-574-3

EUROPE

ASIA

Thailand

AFRICA

AUSTRALIA

ANTARCTICA

△ **Thailand's flag**
King Rama VI designed the red, white, and blue flag in 1917. It is called *Trai rong*, meaning "three colors." Red stands for the lifeblood of the Thai people. White represents the purity of Buddhism, the national religion. The wide blue stripe in the center stands for the monarchy and the importance of the king to the country's people.

THAILAND AT A GLANCE

Area 198,114 square miles (513,115 km^2)

Population 64,631,595

Capital Bangkok, 6,320,174

Other big cities Samut Prakan (390,300), Nonthaburi (291,307), Udon Thani (220,493), Nakhon Ratchasima (204,392), Chiang Mai (167,776), Chon Buri (188,200), Ubon Ratchathani (106,442)

Highest mountain Doi Inthanon, 8,514 feet (2,595 m)

Longest rivers Chao Phraya, 227 miles (366 km); Mekong (part in Thailand), 620 miles (1,000 km)

Largest lake Songkhla, 1,000 square miles (2,600 km^2)

Official language Thai

▽ **Thai stamps** Traditional Thai dancers and a golden Buddah represent Thailand's rich history and culture. Agriculture and modern business technology are also featured.

◁ **Thai money** Thailand's currency is the Baht. There are 100 satang in 1 Baht (written B1). The numbers on the bills are written in both Thai and English. The B50 bill shows King Mongkut, who reigned from 1851 to 1868, and the B100 bill features King Bhumibol Adulyadej, whose reign began in 1946.

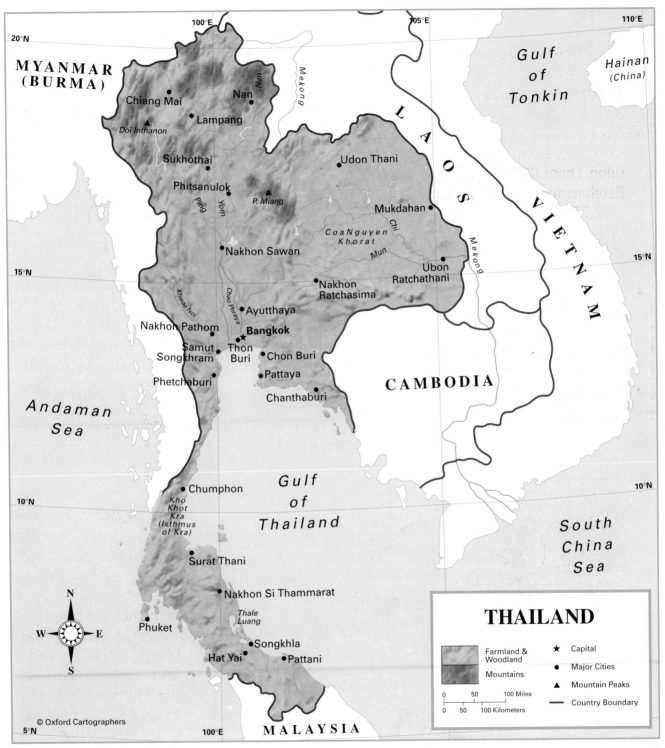

MYANMAR (BURMA)

Chiang Mai
Nan
Lampang
Doi Inthanon
Sukhothai
Phitsanulok
P. Miang
Ping
Yom
Nan
Mekong

LAOS

Udon Thani
Mukdahan
Chi
Co a N g u y e n
K h o r a t
Mun
Nakhon Sawan
Nakhon
Ratchasima
Ubon
Ratchathani
Mekong

VIETNAM

Gulf
of
Tonkin

Hainan
(China)

Khwae Noi
Chao Phraya
Ayutthaya
Nakhon Pathom
Bangkok ★
Samut
Songkhram
Thon
Buri
Chon Buri
Pattaya
Phetchaburi
Chanthaburi

CAMBODIA

Andaman
Sea

Gulf
of
Thailand

South
China
Sea

Chumphon
Kho
Khot
Kra
(Isthmus
of Kra)

Surat Thani

Nakhon Si Thammarat

Thale
Luang
Phuket
Songkhla
Hat Yai
Pattani

N
W E
S

© Oxford Cartographers

MALAYSIA

20°N
100°E
105°E
110°E

15°N

15°N

10°N

10°N

5°N
100°E

THAILAND

Farmland & Woodland	★ Capital
Mountains	● Major Cities
	▲ Mountain Peaks
	— Country Boundary

0   50   100 Miles
0   50   100 Kilometers

5

KINGDOM OF THE FREE

In Southeast Asia, a huge finger of land called a peninsula stretches southward between the Bay of Bengal and the South China Sea. At the heart of the peninsula is the Kingdom of Thailand, once known as the Kingdom of Siam.

In Thailand, it is warm and usually sunny all year. But between May and September, winds called monsoons bring heavy rains. During the wet season, farmers plant rice seeds in the flooded fields. More than three-quarters of Thailand's sixty million people work on the land. Rice is the most important crop.

Thailand is a beautiful country that is rich in wildlife. There are mountains, misty waterfalls, and forests that are home to gibbons (small apes), elephants, and the rare Indochinese tiger. All kinds of exotic fish swim in waters around Thailand's shores. The country's coast is dotted with swamps of mangrove trees. These swamps are the nesting grounds for many birds.

About 2,300 years ago, a religion called Buddhism reached Thailand from India. Ever

▽ **A Buddhist festival** Many festivals are held throughout the year in Thailand. Most of them are religious, have to do with royalty, or are connected with the rice harvest.

△ **The natural beauty of Thailand** Visitors can relax in the shade of coconut palms on beaches fringed by blue-green seas or dive among coral reefs alive with colorful fish.

◁ **The Grand Palace in Bangkok, Thailand's capital** The palace was built in 1782 by King Rama I. The present king does not live here, but it is now used for state occasions.

since then, Buddhism is the most popular religion among the Thai people. Everywhere, you will see statues of the Buddha, Buddhist monks with shaved heads, and Buddhist temples with tiered roofs. You can visit the ruins of temples built by kings who lived centuries ago. Today, Thailand still has a king and a royal family, but there is also a prime minister, who is elected by the people.

In the Thai language, "Thai" means "free," so "Thailand" is "land of the free." Thai is a very old language with its own alphabet. But street names and signs are written in both the Thai and English alphabets. Thai people are known for their friendliness and will always help you find your way around. You can travel across the country in buses, trains, and airplanes.

CITY OF ANGELS

The capital of Thailand is Bangkok. The Thai people call it Krung Thep, which means "City of Angels." Bangkok lies not far from the mouth of the Chao Phraya River and spreads across both riverbanks. With nearly six million people living there, it is by far the largest and busiest city in Thailand. It is also the country's largest port.

Among Bangkok's modern skyscrapers are wonderful temples. The Thai word for "temple" is *wat*. One of the city's best-known temples, the Wat Phra Kaeo, stands on the grounds of the Grand Palace, on the east bank of the river. Its green and orange tiled roofs and gleaming curved spires give it a magical appearance. This beautiful temple houses a small jade statue called the Emerald Buddha, which is sacred to Buddhists. The air in the temple is filled with the scent of flowers and incense because so many Buddhists use these as part of their worship. Just across the river is the Wat Arun, or Temple of Dawn. It is the city's most famous landmark. The central tower, covered in porcelain, rises to 258 feet (79 m) above the riverbank.

Thai people usually carry an amulet, or good-luck charm, with them. You can choose a lucky charm at Bangkok's amulet market. Here, you will find more than 100 stalls with local people making or selling miniature dolls, Buddhas, or other images in wood, clay, or gold.

A short distance downriver from Wat Arun is Chinatown, where most of the city's Chinese people live. It is a fascinating maze of alleyways with bazaars that sell everything from spices to electronic toys. If you prefer elegant shopping malls and wide streets, head for downtown Bangkok. Here you can buy Thai silk, gemstones, and traditional rattan furniture, as well as the latest fashions.

▽ **Tuk-tuk in Bangkok** Taking one of these three-wheeled, open-sided taxis is one of the best ways to get around the city's crowded streets.

△ **View of Bangkok from Lumphini Park** Glass and concrete skyscrapers form an impressive skyline high above the rooftops of Buddhist temples.

◁ **A Thai restaurant in Bangkok** Spicy curries, tasty stir-fried chicken and prawns (large shrimps), noodles, fried rice, and soups are all part of the Thai menu.

TRADE AND INDUSTRY

The traditional way of shopping all over Thailand is to bargain over the price, but to do so calmly and with a smile. Visiting the open-air markets at Chatuchak, on the outskirts of Bangkok, will give you plenty of practice in this ancient skill. Whatever you want—from handmade umbrellas to a pair of jeans—you will find it somewhere among Chatuchak's 6,000 market stands.

From Bangkok you can also take a day trip to the town of Nonthaburi. Arriving by river, you will see houses on stilts and people living on huge teak (hardwood) barges that are used for carrying rice. Nonthaburi is famous for its beautiful flowers and its durian fruit. Durian looks like a spiky green football and has a strong smell. Its yellow-and-white flesh has a tangy, nutty taste.

▽ **Wat Pikul Tong** This splendid temple with its golden Buddha stands on the banks of the Noi River in the Tachang District. It is one of many beautiful temples in Thailand.

△ **Handicraft center in Bangkok** Brightly painted umbrellas made of silk, cotton, or mulberry paper make wonderful souvenirs for tourists looking for Thai handicrafts.

10

Waterways have always been important to the Thais. A network of canals existed in Bangkok long before the streets were built. Today, people who live in Bangkok on the west bank of the Chao Phraya River still use the canals. You can see them paddling their canoes, selling fruit and flowers as they have done for centuries.

Taking the coast road going east from the outskirts of Bangkok offers a different view of Thailand. You will pass huge oil and gas refineries, as well as the popular seaside resort of Pattaya, before reaching a fascinating town called Chanthaburi.

For 500 years, the hills around Chanthaburi have been mined for rubies and sapphires. People came from all over the world in hopes of striking it rich. Today, you can watch the gem dealers in their shop windows picking through piles of precious stones and examining them through an eyeglass. Some dealers also cut and polish the stones. Thai gemcutters are some of the most skilled in the world.

▽ **Traditional wooden houses** Many people in Thailand who live beside the water build their homes on stilts. These houses are on a canal bank in Bangkok.

FRIENDS AND NEIGHBORS

Take a trip on an air-conditioned bus north from Chanthaburi. Ahead, on the other side of the cloud-covered mountains, lies the dry scrubland of Thailand's northeast plateau. After a journey of about six hours, you will arrive at Nakhon Ratchasima. This busy town with crowded narrow streets is known as the "gateway to the northeast."

Thailand's northeast is called Isaan. Most of the famous Thai silk is made by the women of the villages of Isaan. Silkworms feed on the leaves of the mulberry trees that grow here in the crumbly sandstone soil. First, the silk moth lays her eggs, which develop into silkworms. These then form cocoons, wrapping themselves in a long thread that is produced from their mouths. The Thai women collect the silk threads and weave them into cloth.

Scattered across the region, you will find wonderful ruins of ancient Prasats. In these stone Khmer-style shrines, people honored and worshiped Indian and local territorial gods and the Lord Buddha.

The largest one, Prasat Hin Phimai, is in Phimai, a little town on the Mun River. The pinkish-brown and cream-colored stone temple buildings and the delicate carvings of gods and demons on the temple's staircases and doorways have all been beautifully restored.

The railroad from Nakhon Ratchasima goes as far east as the large town of Ubon Ratchathani. From there, you can catch a bus to the easternmost point of Thailand. This is where the Mun River meets the mighty Mekong River. The Mekong forms the border between northeastern Thailand and the neighboring country of Laos. At the border town of Nong Khai, a modern bridge spans the river between the two countries. It is called Friendship Bridge.

▷ **Selling silk** Thai silk is renowned for its thickness and sheen. Two-ply silk is made into dresses and skirts. Heavier, four-ply silk is used for making suits.

12

◁ **Thai boxing** Boxers can use their feet as well as their fists in this traditional sport. Thai boxing is popular all over the country, with provinces such as Isaan holding competitions that are shown on national television.

▽ **Candle Festival at Ubon Ratchathani** In July, people parade through town with wax sculptures mounted on floats to celebrate this Buddhist festival. The people here are also honoring King Bhumibol Adulyadej.

IN THE FAR NORTH

In 1996, one of the world's oldest dinosaur fossils was discovered in northeastern Thailand. You can see the fossil remains near the town of Khon Kaen in the park where the discovery was made. This dinosaur lived 120 million years ago!

There are flights from Khon Kaen to Chiang Mai in the northern region. For more than 700 years, Chiang Mai has been the north's most important city. It is thought of as Thailand's second city, after Bangkok, though with fewer than 200,000 people, it is tiny compared with the capital.

Chiang Mai nestles in a green valley among mountains, on the banks of the Ping River. A moat surrounds the old town district, which has fine temples and wooden houses.

To Thai people, the new year starts in April. If you are in Chiang Mai at that time, be prepared for a soaking. People here celebrate by building sand castles shaped like temple towers and holding water fights. There are street parades with marchers carrying cleaned and polished statues of Buddha, which also get drenched!

The city is famous for its handicrafts. You will find fascinating stores and workshops selling lacquered bamboo trays, silver jewelry, and carved wooden elephants inlaid with sparkling glass. You can also buy sculptures made of jade and beautiful green-glazed pottery called celadon.

Eating here is as exciting as shopping. Try the delicious Chiang Mai curry, a recipe of pork flavored with ginger, garlic, and pork fat. Northern Thai cooking is quite similar in style to Burmese, with lots of rich curries and soups. In fact, Chiang Mai lies just 70 miles (110 km) from the border with Myanmar, the country that used to be called Burma.

▷ **Golden temple** This beautiful temple sits atop Doi Suthep, a mountain on the western edge of Chiang Mai. From the temple grounds there is a good view of the city.

△ **Making silverware in Chiang Mai** Local silversmiths heat, hammer, and engrave the precious metal to produce beautiful silver cups, bowls, plates, and jewelry.

▽ **Elephant ride near Chiang Mai** Elephants were once used to move stones for building temples and to carry lumber. Today they mostly carry tourists on rides in the forest.

THE NORTHERN HIGHLANDS

Doi Inthanon is the country's highest mountain. It rises 8,514 feet (2,595 m) in a northern highland wilderness of forest and waterfalls. The forests are alive with the calls of birds and the hooting of gibbons.

From Chiang Mai, the highway twists through the mountains toward Mae Hong Son. This town of 6,000 people began 170 years ago as a camp where wild elephants were trained for logging and for use in battle.

▽ **Waterfall in Doi Inthanon National Park**
The most spectacular waterfall is Mae Ya, one of the highest waterfalls in Thailand.

Hilltribes live in the region between Chiang Mai, Mae Hong Son, and Chiang Rai, to the northeast. The Thais call them *chao khao*, meaning "mountain people." The largest hilltribe is the Karen, who came from Myanmar and China in the 1600s. The oldest is the Lawa, who came from Cambodia some 1,200 years ago.

You can trek through jungles and go rafting down rivers to villages where the hilltribes live. But take a guide with you and be sure to respect the native customs. If you don't, village officials may fine you, as they fine their own people who break the rules.

△ **Hilltribe people** About 750,000 people live in Thailand's many hilltribe villages. The main hilltribes are the Karen, Hmong, Yao, Lisu, Akha, and Lawa. They each have their own customs, religion, and language.

◁ **A farmer near Chiang Rai** Farmers use water buffaloes to plow the fields before planting. After harvesting, these large animals trample on the rice crop to separate the grain.

Not far from Chiang Rai are the ruins of the old city of Chiang Saen. The ruins stand alongside the modern town in the valley of the Mekong River. Giant catfish live in this river. The biggest ones can be 10 feet (3 m) long and weigh as much as 660 pounds (300 kg). The fishing season here begins in April.

BIRTH OF A NATION

Highway 1 leads southward from Chiang Rai through the historic town of Lampang. Buses arrive here headed for Mae Sot, a small town near the border with Myanmar. Mae Sot is home to Thais, Burmese, and some Karen and Hmong hilltribes.

Farther south lies the village of Umphang. Here, the Tee Lor Su Waterfall plunges down in three spectacular leaps. No buses pass this way, but you can arrive by *songthaew*—an open-ended truck, where passengers sit on two rows of benches facing each other. The road climbs steeply as it winds its way around narrow overhanging ledges toward the village and waterfall.

The road east from Mae Sot passes the ancient city of Sukhothai. Here, more than 750 years ago, two Thai generals and their armies drove out the Khmers, who ruled the northern plains, and started the Sukhothai kingdom. Sukhothai's third and greatest king was Ramkhamhaeng. He invented the alphabet that forms the basis of written Thai.

The ruins of the ancient city, with its many temples, are spread over a wide area. Every year here the people of modern Sukhothai celebrate the end of the rainy season. They make little boats from banana leaves, decorate them with flowers, and attach lighted candles. Then, by the light of the full moon, they float the candlelit boats on the ponds among the temple ruins.

Across the fertile plains to the south is an even older town. Lop Buri was founded more than 1,400 years ago. Today, the town is famous for the monkeys in its center. It is also home to a sacred stone footprint that is said to have been made by the Lord Buddha himself.

▽ **The Wat Phra Kaeo Don Tao in Lampang**
This lovely old temple, built in the 1600s, once housed the Emerald Buddha, which is now in Bangkok.

▷ **Green rice paddies** The well-watered plains, which cover central Thailand, are known as "the rice bowl." Most of the country's food is grown here.

▽ **Boat racing in Phichit** To celebrate the end of the rainy season, the people of Phichit, a town on Thailand's northern plains, hold boat races on the Nan River.

MONUMENTS OLD AND NEW

In 1351, a prince from Lop Buri founded Ayutthaya as the new Thai capital. By the mid-1600s, Ayutthaya was a city of a million people and the capital of an empire. Then, in 1767, Burmese armies invaded, destroying the city and ending the empire.

Ayutthaya was built on an island between the Chao Phraya, Lop Buri, and Pa Sak Rivers. Today, the ruins of the ancient city share the island with modern buildings. Here, you will find the remains of dozens of old temples made of red brick and gray stone. Many of them, with their sharp spires and tall towers, are still standing.

Nakhon Pathom is much older still. More than 2,000 years ago, the Mon people, who lived in the south of Myanmar and in the Chao Phraya Basin, settled here. You will

▽ **Bridge over the Khwae Noi** This steel bridge was built by prisoners of the Japanese during World War II.

still find families of Mon people living in western Thailand around the towns of Kanchanaburi and Ratchaburi. When Buddhism was introduced to Thailand, it began in Nakhon Pathom. Today, in the center of town, the world's highest Buddhist temple tower—a 380-foot- (39-m-) high golden dome and spire—honors the event.

The bridge over the Khwae Noi River at Kanchanaburi is part of a monument from recent times. In 1942, during World War II, the Japanese forced many Western prisoners of war and others to build a railroad linking Kanchanaburi with the town of Thanbyuzayat in Myanmar. It took just fifteen months to complete the job, but more than 100,000 prisoners died doing so.

You can still travel along part of that railroad line today. The two-hour train ride takes you across the Khwae Noi River bridge, through a narrow pass that the prisoners dug out of solid rock, and over a trestle bridge built along the sheer face of a cliff.

◁ **Wat Yai Chai Mongkol at Ayutthaya** This magnificent temple was built in 1357.

▽ **Floating market, near Ratchaburi** Women sell vegetables, fruit, and flowers to people who live along the canal banks.

GOING SOUTH

A long neck of land stretches from south of Bangkok to Thailand's border with Malaysia. The blue waters of the Gulf of Thailand—part of the South China Sea—lap the sandy beaches on the eastern side. Here, most of the rain falls between October and January. This differs from Thailand's normal weather.

The climate suits the tall sweet-sapped palm trees that grow all over Phetchaburi Province. Sugar is squeezed from these plants to make *khanom*—delicious and brightly colored Thai candy. The historic old town of Phetchaburi, capital of the province, is famous for its candymaking.

Farther south, in the fall, the coastal mudflats at the foot of the cliffs swarm with hundreds of different kinds of migrating birds. And in the nearby freshwater marsh, the rare purple heron and other wading birds make their nests.

The official "gateway to the south" is Chumphon. This lively town lies in a region that may be battered by typhoons—violent storms that can cause flooding, flatten homes, and uproot thousands of rubber trees, coconut palms, and banana trees.

Two boats a day leave Chumphon for Ko Tao Island. From here and the bigger island Ko Samui, you can go scuba-diving and explore the magical undersea world of coral reefs and brilliantly colored fish. These waters are also home to dolphins and *pla thu*, the short-bodied mackerel, which is a common part of the Thais' diet.

Back on the mainland, the town of Nakhon Si Thammarat is worth visiting. It is famous for its handicrafts and a Buddhist temple with a gold-leaf spire. It is also the home of the "shadow-puppet" theater. You can watch the leather puppets being made and see how they are projected onto a screen to produce the "shadow" effect.

◁ **Basketmaking** This young woman is skillfully weaving the stems of different ferns to make a basket. The town of Nakhon Si Thammarat is known for its basketware.

△ **Rugged scenery on Ko Samui** This island in the Gulf of Thailand can be reached by ferry from various ports in the Surat Thani region. It lies about 10 miles from the mainland.

◁ **An assortment of khanom—Thai candy** Palm sugar is used in making Thai candy and is an ingredient in many Thai desserts.

BORDER COUNTRY

Phatthalung is a bustling southern town set dramatically among hills and mountains. It was once a favorite hideout for bandits. Today, most visitors come here to go boating in the Thale Noi Waterbird Park, a freshwater lagoon where white egrets and other species of waterbirds nest among the matted reeds and lotus pads.

Farther south, at Songkhla, the lagoon meets the Gulf of Thailand. Here, on the beach at the edge of town, you will see many brightly painted prawn-fishing boats with dragon-head bows ringed with flowers. Many Muslims live in southern Thailand, and these boats belong to Muslim fishermen. Muslims follow the Islam religion and worship in a building called a mosque.

Down the coast, the old town of Pattani has both Thai and Chinese temples, as well as the ruins of a famous brick mosque with no roof. It was started in the 1500s, but after a series of mishaps, including being struck by lightning, the mosque was never finished.

Southern Thai Muslims breed doves for luck. You will often see a birdcage hanging outside their homes. Every spring, the town of Yala holds a competition to find the finest and most musical birds. Breeders come from all over Southeast Asia to take part and show off their prized pets.

Yala lies inland, on the main road from Pattani to Betong, a town on the border with Malaysia. You can also reach the border if

△ **Shell beans** Beans are one of Thailand's many vegetable crops. Thanks to the tropical climate, Thai farmers can grow a wide variety of fruit and vegetables.

you follow the coast road from Pattani. The road passes through Narathiwat, a sleepy town where cows and goats roam the streets.

From the western coast of southern Thailand, you can take a ferry to explore Ko Tarutao and its many neighboring islands. Here, you will find rain forests and mountains overlooking sandy bays. Between September and April, leatherback and other turtles come ashore to lay their eggs in the sand.

Wild pigs The forests of Ko Tarutao are home to wild pigs, crab-eating macaques (a kind of monkey), mouse deer, rare breeds of squirrels, and many other animals.

Muslims in southern Thailand Muslims traditionally wear long robes, and the women cover their heads. Many of the Thai Muslims who live near the border with Malaysia speak a language that is similar to Malay.

ISLANDS IN THE SUN

Forests of mangrove trees grow along the fringes of Thailand's west coast. You can hire a boat to take you through the mangrove swamps around the fishing town of Krabi. At low tide, the mass of tangled roots supporting the mangrove trees can be seen above the waterline. Mudfish and sharp-clawed fiddler crabs make their homes here. Kingfisher birds and sea eagles come here to feed.

From Krabi, catch a ferry to the nearby islands. The beautiful turquoise waters off the west coast are crystal clear. In the distance you can see tall, strange-shaped limestone rocks jutting out of the sea. To get a closer look at some of these rocks and caves, take a tour around Phang Nga Bay.

Thailand's biggest and most popular island is Phuket. Tourist hotels overlook sun-drenched beaches on the island's western shores. On December 26, 2004, a powerful tsunami (giant waves caused by an earthquake) struck Phuket and other parts of the west coast. More than 5,000 people died.

A large group of *Chao Le*, or "sea people," live on Phuket. The Chao Le speak their own language and have their own customs. Some make their living by fearlessly diving deep into the sea for pearls and shells. They are also experts at scaling high cliffs to gather the nests of sea swifts. The nests are sold to the Chinese for making bird's-nest soup, a Chinese delicacy.

Your tour of Thailand is nearly over. But, before you leave, be sure to visit Khao Sok National Park back on the mainland. Here, you can go on a jungle safari at dusk. Look out for elephants, prowling tigers, or clouded leopards. And you can spend your last night in Thailand in a treehouse.

▷ **Buddhist monks on Phuket** Most Thai boys and young men spend some time as a monk. Monks may not own anything. They depend entirely on what is given to them.

△ **Fish farming in coastal waters** Not all fish are caught from the sea. Some fish, including many shellfish, are bred in tanks in sheltered bays.

▽ **Children in the Ko Surin Islands, off Thailand's west coast** Clear waters, sandy beaches, and forest scenery attract tourists to the islands.

THAILAND FACTS AND FIGURES

People
More than half of Thailand's people are ethnic Thais. Some of the others, such as Lao, Malay, Khmer, and Burmese, have their origins in countries on Thailand's borders. The Mon of Central Thailand are an ancient people who came from Mongolia. Still others are descended from Chinese or Indian settlers.

Trade and Industry
Much of Thailand's wealth is from tourism. More than 6 million people visit every year. Manufactured goods are also a major source of income. Tin, rubber, lead, and gypsum are among the country's natural resources. Oil and natural gas are also found. Thailand's biggest trading partners are the United States, Japan, China, Malaysia, and Singapore.

Farming
Nearly two-thirds of the labor force work on the land. Most are rice farmers. Rice is the country's biggest crop and export. Farmers

△ **Wat Phra Kaeo in Bangkok** This royal temple area is filled with buildings of beautiful shapes and colors, and with statues of characters that act as guards over the shrines.

also grow sugarcane, tapioca, corn, soybeans, and jute as well as tomatoes, peppers, mangoes, bananas, and other fruits and vegetables. In the south, there are rubber tree plantations. Horses and water buffaloes are kept as work animals. Chickens, pigs, and cattle are raised for meat.

Fishing
Thai people eat a variety of fish and shellfish. Mackerel, mullet, snapper, crawfish, octopus, squid, prawns, shrimps, and mussels are among the catch from the sea. Carp and other freshwater fish are taken from the rivers. The Mekong River has the world's largest catfish.

Food
Thais usually eat with a fork and spoon instead of chopsticks. Here are some Thai dishes:
Tom khaa Kai A thick soup made with chicken, coconut milk, and fish sauce, flavored with lemon grass, chili, and coriander
Pat phak lai yang Broccoli, peas, asparagus, carrots, mushrooms, and bean sprouts stir-fried with chili and soy sauce
Sangkhaya fakhtong Steamed pumpkin with an egg-and-coconut cream filling

Schools
Children attend school from the ages of seven to fifteen. Education in the public schools is free. After secondary school, some students who pass their exams go on to

higher education. They can attend a university, an institute of technology, or a college for training teachers.

Media

Hundreds of newspapers and magazines are published in the Thai language. The biggest-selling one is *Thai Rath*. There are also some in Chinese. *Bangkok Post* and *The Nation* are popular English-language daily newspapers.

On television, Channels 3, 5, 7, 9 and 11 broadcast programs throughout the country. Thailand has 15 Internet service providers and 1.2 million Internet users. Radio Thailand broadcasts news, sports, and other programs in both Thai and English. There are also music programs on the radio.

Drama and Music

Classical Thai drama takes the form of music and dance. The dancers act out the stories from ancient legends, accompanied by

△ **Traditional Thai dancing** Dancers in elaborate costumes and headdresses act out a drama based on an ancient legend. This form of dance is called *khon*.

traditional music. They wear tall headdresses, embroidered silk costumes, and masks. The dancers do not speak, but a chorus offstage sings about what is happening. Modern Thai music is often a blend of traditional styles, folk music, and western rock

music. Some bands use ancient instruments, such as the *khaen* (bamboo mouth organ) or *ching* (small cymbals), as well as electric guitars.

Festivals

Some festivals include noisy, colorful parades, when the people can enjoy themselves. Others are quieter and more solemn. There are festivals throughout the year. Here are a few of them:

February–April **Kite-flying contests** Across the country, kite-flyers compete against each other.

May **Raek Na Kwan or Royal Plowing Ceremony, performed at Sanam Luang** Watched by the king, men in ceremonial dress parade with oxen and the royal plow to mark the start of the rice season.

May **Visakha Puja** (full-moon day) Buddhists celebrate the Buddha's birth, life, and death, ending with a candlelit procession around the temple.

29

THAILAND FACTS AND FIGURES

Literature

Thai literature dates back to the 1200s, when the Thai alphabet was invented.

The first writings in Thailand were religious, influenced by Buddhism. Later, writers told legends and adventure stories such as *Ramayama*, an epic tale that came from India. Modern-day novelists like Atsiri Thammachoat and Khamsing Srinawk often choose subjects closer to home, such as how the lives of Thai peasant farmers are changing.

Art

Traditionally, Thailand's art and religion are closely related. The fine sculptures from ancient Sukhothai include some statues of the Buddha walking. At the same time, Sukhothai potters made beautiful celadon plates. Celadon plates have a green glaze and are decorated with chrysanthemum and fish designs.

Temples from the Ayutthaya period have red-and-cream murals (wall paintings) of the Buddha.

△ **Pigtailed macaque** The agile animal can easily climb the tallest trees in the forest. In southern Thailand, pigtailed macaques are sometimes trained to pick coconuts.

Religion

More than 90 percent of Thais are Buddhists. Buddhists believe in peace and in doing no harm. They also believe that after they die, they will be reborn, perhaps as another person or as an animal. Most other Thais are either Muslim, Christian, or Hindu. Hinduisim, like Buddhism, came to Thailand from India.

Sports

Muay Thai (Thai boxing) is the sport with the biggest following. Another traditional sport is *takraw*, a ball game. Thais also enjoy playing or watching golf, soccer, badminton, and tennis.

Plants

Hardwood trees, including teak, make up most of Thailand's forests. These are deciduous trees—ones that shed their leaves. This enables them to use less water during the dry season. In the south, there are tropical rain forests, orchids, lianas, and ferns.

Animals

Thailand has more than 250 species of mammals. Macaque monkeys and gibbons live in forests or national parks across the country. Deer, wild pigs, and tapirs are also found there. Elephants are rare in the wild. Tigers and the clouded leopard are rarer still. Snakes include the venomous banded krait, mangrove snake, and the reticulated python. Hornbills, sea eagles, and rare birds such as the pitta are among Thailand's 900 bird varieties. Sharks, manta rays, barracudas, and other fish swim off the coast.

HISTORY

People have lived on the land that is now Thailand for 40,000 years. Over time, these prehistoric hunters learned to farm and built settlements. By 2000 B.C., they were making bronze tools. In the next centuries, Mons, Khmers, and early Thais arrived, and Buddhism also came to Thailand.

In the A.D. 1200s, the Thais defeated the Khmers and Chinese invaders, and started the first Thai kingdom, at Sukhothai. Art and culture flourished there. Later, a new, more powerful Thai kingdom arose at Ayutthaya.

Ayutthaya grew through trade and conquest, but was destroyed by the Burmese in 1767. Soon afterward, another new Thai kingdom began at Thon Buri, opposite present-day Bangkok. King Rama I moved the capital to its present location in 1782. Thailand prospered through trade with Britain, France, and the United States.

In the 1930s, the king gave up some of his power, and elections were held for a prime minister.

During World War II, Japanese soldiers were stationed in Thailand. After the war, Thailand held its first full elections, with different political parties running for office. Since then, there have been other elected governments, as well as takeovers by the army. King Bhumibol Adulyadej, known as Rama IX, became king in 1946. Thaksin Shinawatra became prime minister in 2001. Over the next several years, he was heavily criticized and was overthrown in 2006.

LANGUAGE

Thai is a very old language. People in different regions speak completely different dialects. Thai has its own alpahabet of 76 letters. On this page, the English alphabet is used to represent Thai sounds. When you speak to a stranger in Thai, you should end your sentence with "khrap" if you are male, or "kha" if you are female. This is a form of politeness, and is always used with such greetings as "hello."

Useful words and phrases

English	Thai
Zero	suun
One	neung
Two	sawng
Three	saam
Four	sli
Five	haa
Six	hok
Seven	jet
Eight	paet
Nine	kao
Ten	sip
Sunday	wan artit
Monday	wan chan

Useful words and phrases

English	Thai
Tuesday	wan angkaan
Wednesday	wan phut
Thursday	wan paruhat
Friday	wan suk
Saturday	wan sao
Hello	sawatdii khrap/kha
Good Morning	sawatdii khrap/kha
Good Night	sawatdii khrap/kha
Please	prawd
Thank you	khwap khun

INDEX

Acknowledgments
Book created for Highlights for Children, Inc. by Bender Richardson White.
Editors: Lionel Bender and Belinda Weber
Designer: Mike Pilley, Radius
Art Editor: Ben White
Picture Researchers: Cathy Stastny, Daniela Marceddu
Production: Kim Richardson

Maps produced by Oxford Cartographers, England.
Banknotes from MRI Bankers Guide to Foreign Currency.
Stamps courtesy of Scott Publishing Co., Sidney, OH 45365 (www.scottonline.com).

Editorial Consultant: Andrew Gutelle
Guide to Thailand is approved by the Tourism Authority of Thailand, London
Thailand Consultant: Ajarn Somboon Singkamanan
Managing Editor, Highlights New Products: Margie Hayes Richmond

Picture credits
Corbis = Corbis Images UK, DAS = David Simson/DAS Photographs, JDTP = James Davis Travel Photography, TAT = Tourism Authority of Thailand, TL = The Travel Library. t = top, b = bottom, l = left, r = right.
Cover: JDTA. 6: TAT. 7t: TL/Ben Davies. 7b: TTA. 8, 9t: JDTP. 9b: Corbis/Kevin R. Morris. 10l: TAT. 10r, 11: JDTP. 12: TAT. 13t: JDTP. 13b, 14-15, 15t, 15b, 16: TAT. 17t: JDTP. 17b: TAT. 18: Corbis/Kevin R. Morris. 19t, 19b: TAT. 20: Corbis/David Cumming. 21l: JDTP. 21r: TAT. 22, 23t, 23b: TAT. 24: JDTP. 25t, 25b: DAS. 26-27, 27t: JDTP. 27b: TAT. 28: TL/R. Richardson. 29: TAT. 30: Oxford Scientific Films/Daniel J. Cox. *Illustration on page 1* by Tom Powers.